Reiki Journeys

STORIES OF PERSONAL AND SPIRITUAL GROWTH THROUGH REIKI

EDITED BY

Yvonne P. Gleason, RMT

REIKI SANCTUARY OF NORTHERN VIRGINIA

DISCLAIMER: Reiki is not a substitute for professional medical care, medical diagnosis, or medical treatment. Reiki sessions are given to help with relaxation and stress reduction to promote well-being. Reiki practitioners do not diagnose conditions, nor do they prescribe or perform medical treatment or interfere with the treatment of a licensed medical professional. For any ailment that one may have, it is recommended that one receive care from a licensed health-care or medical professional.

ISBN: 978-0-9896713-0-9

Published by:
Reiki Sanctuary of Northern Virginia
PO Box 232192, Centreville, VA 20120-2192
www.ReikiNorthernVirginia.com

A special thank you to Kathleen Strattan for her proofreading services
Text design and composition by John Reinhardt Book Design

Printed in the United States of America

A portion of the proceeds from the sale of this book will be donated to the Life with Cancer Family Center's Reiki treatment program.

In gratitude for the journey.

Contents

Our Journeys

More about Reiki

Reiki: A Brief Definition

REIKI IS AN ENERGY modality that promotes deep relaxation, wellness, clarity, focus, personal growth, and spiritual growth.

Reiki means "universal life force" or "universal life energy." This energy comes from the universe or Source through the practitioner to the recipient for his or her well-being.

Reiki is administered with the practitioner's hands just above or lightly placed on the recipient's clothed body in prescribed hand positions.

Reiki helps to restore balance on many energetic levels: physical, emotional, mental, and spiritual. In turn, this promotes wellness which can enable growth and development in all personal and spiritual aspects of daily life.

The Reiki Ideals*

Just for Today, I will...

Let go of anger

Let go of worry

Be grateful

Let my work be honest work

Be kind to others.

*This is a modified version of the Reiki Ideals based on the version believed to have been used by Mikao Usui.

Introduction

REIKI JOURNEYS is a gathering of voices, a sharing of experiences from those who have grown personally and spiritually through Reiki.

Some of the stories speak to the ability of Reiki to help one find focus, clarity, and life purpose. Other stories unveil a discovery of something greater than "self" with a deeper connection to an all-embracing Higher Power. Still, some stories reveal a development of intuition through Reiki and how that gift can help others.

Reiki has provided a path for my own personal and spiritual growth. I've always felt unconditionally loved when I've received Reiki treatments. I usually feel a sense of calm and I am better able to focus on daily tasks and easily make decisions.

As a child, I gave Reiki to my skinned knees and paper cuts, holding my hand over the hurt areas, allowing the light from the universe to come through to help me heal.

But as time went on, I got distracted by school and social events, and I let the Reiki go for a long time. It wasn't until I was an adult that I came across a book on Reiki. When I opened it up, I began to read about what I'd been doing for myself as a child.

I began to receive regular Reiki treatments. Each time I received Reiki, I felt more deeply connected to Source, and in turn, that allowed everything else in my daily life to flow more smoothly. I knew I wanted to share this wonderful modality of Reiki with others.

Eventually, I was guided to become certified as a Reiki Master/Teacher which helped me to utilize more efficiently the Reiki for myself and for others.

I believe that giving Reiki and teaching Reiki helps us to become more aware of our connection to the universal energy and the Divine within. Once we have that awareness, we may find that it's easier for everything in our daily lives to fall into place as we grow and move forward.

Many find that personal and spiritual growth go hand in hand. In the process of growing, some form of healing usually occurs, whether it's physical, emotional, mental, or spiritual. Many times, the journey itself is the healing.

May these Reiki stories inspire you as you travel along your own unique journey!

Many Reiki blessings,

Yvonne P. Gleason, RMT
Reiki Sanctuary of Northern Virginia

Our Journeys

"I asked . . . for my life to be more about living."

—M. A. HOOVER

My Journey into Unconditional Love

BY M. A. HOOVER

I WAS FIFTY YEARS OLD and bulimia had been my "curse" for twenty-five years. Often, I felt like a shell of a person, a useless human being. I was lost and consumed by my addiction, and I felt the need to punish myself for whatever the reason was on that particular day. I'd push food into my mouth with the full intention of enjoying every bite but with the knowledge that soon all my pain would be spewing back out. I lied to my family and to myself about my personal struggle and thought that I would eventually have to stop or die. Every day was a challenge to find a way not to think about my "power." I gave my "power" a huge existence in my life. I wrote about it and made reference to it as I talked out loud to myself, and I gave it an ugly form that overtook me. I'd given my own personal strength and power over to the addiction, and now, the addiction had power over me.

I have a wonderful husband and two children I love more than myself. But this was my secret and only my secret that nobody would understand. After all, what would my family think about me throwing up all the time just to lose weight? So I didn't tell my family. I suffered alone and felt very isolated. Thoughts of food consumed me.

A positive self-image was what I lacked, and no matter how many people said nice things to me, I would look in the mirror and see nothing that appealed to me. Nothing about me was good enough. There was nothing that I could be proud of, absolutely nothing. I knew there were counseling groups on food addiction, but, of course, "those people" were really sick, not me.

Searching for some hope, I finally found Reiki. By then, I was open to anything that might release me from this "power." Before the session, I talked with my practitioner, and I let her know everything about me. I cried and complained and asked for help. She explained the process of Reiki. I was drawn in by the thought of someone who could understand me and want to help me.

After the session, I was able to relate to my practitioner what I'd felt: the overall comfort like a warm blanket surrounding me. She told me what she had perceived at the energy centers of my body. Over time, I learned about loving angelic energies and guides that I could call upon. I was happy to know that she could call upon these helpers at the beginning of my Reiki sessions. I also learned about crystals that resonated with my energy, and unconditional love.

Before my experience with Reiki, I'd felt that if there was a God or Higher Power, he wasn't interested in helping poor, little me. After all, there was a huge world to comfort. I was just one person.

As my Reiki sessions continued, my outlook shifted. I began to make time in my daily life to sit, meditate, think, and ask for help. I asked my Higher Power out loud, in writing, and in my dreams for my life to be more about living. I received a profound sense of calmness through my Reiki sessions. I have lost the "need" to punish myself with food. My mind doesn't even cross that line anymore. I am more patient and less stressed, and I look forward to each and every day with hope and determination that I will be happy.

I've found that my intuition has grown, and I listen to my inner voice with more patience. I'd always been told that I was very intuitive, but I had not listened to that inner voice until I found Reiki.

I am an amateur quilter, and I made a quilt with the beautiful colors that my practitioner saw in my aura during one of my Reiki treatment sessions. I bring that quilt with me and cover myself in its beauty at every session.

My life has changed. Reiki has brought me knowledge of myself and ways that I can heal and become more balanced. Now I see the sun come out and notice the warmth that it gives to me. I lie on the grass and feel a connection to the trees . . . the branches…a bird nest…and the life within that nest. When taking walks, I notice the beauty all around me. It is sometimes hard to explain the relief that I feel not having to be "perfect" in my own eyes and to find that even with my "faults," I do love myself.

About the Contributor

M. A. Hoover is a juvenile probation officer in Virginia. She enjoys reading, baking, and spending time with her family and her dog, Toby.

"I felt a warm, loving presence behind me..."

—DAWN WHEELER

A Gift for My Father

BY DAWN WHEELER

IT WAS A WARM FRIDAY in September 2010. Mom and I were waiting for Dad to pick us up at the airport after our flight from France. Dad had said he would be there at 5:00 p.m. and if we weren't outside, he would circle around until we were able to meet him. So we watched and waited as the cars circled and passed. We had arrived a little before 5:00 p.m. Fifteen minutes later, Dad still hadn't shown up. We called. No answer. Another fifteen minutes came—and still no sign of Dad. At 5:45 p.m., I decided to call a neighbor, who said that all the cars were still in the driveway. We then knew something was wrong.

The neighbors found Dad in the bathtub barely conscious but alive. They called the ambulance, and we flagged a cab and headed straight to the hospital. When we got to the hospital, the doctor told us that Dad had suffered a hemorrhagic stroke in his midbrain. The doctors didn't want to give us unrealistic hope. As they prepared Dad for transport to another hospital, I squeezed his hand and told him we were there and that I loved him.

Over the next couple of days, Dad was brought in and out of a coma in the ICU as his brain swelled. I prayed for him. I knew he couldn't see me, probably couldn't hear me, and probably couldn't feel me on his right side. But I thought that maybe, if I held his left hand, if I touched his forehead, he would know he wasn't alone. I was new to Reiki, and I didn't know if it would work for Dad or not. Still, I visualized the healing Reiki going into his body.

Dad pulled out of his coma early, and his physicians seemed surprised. He could read and speak a little, and he even reminded me to file for unemployment, as I had recently been laid off. The doctors had no idea what kind of condition he would be in, but one of the physicians came into his room wanting to shake the hand of the man who defied the odds. Dad was still paralyzed, couldn't swallow, and couldn't control his bodily functions, but his mind, for the most part, was intact and so was his amazing will to live.

As Dad progressed, I wanted to help him with the Reiki. What I didn't expect was how Reiki would help *me*. As I continued to give him Reiki, I was better able to feel the healing, loving energy from the universe. I noticed I began to feel more loving and lighter in my attitude, as if a weight was being lifted from me. I was growing spiritually.

Whenever I gave Reiki to Dad, he would drift into a peaceful sleep. For three months, he made amazing progress, which included a visit home for a day. Dad was recovering.

Then things took a turn. Dad started to develop blood clots. There was no way of treating them without risking further brain damage or death, and Dad made the decision to come home for good. On January 9, he became unconscious, and listening to his breathing, I sensed that the end was near.

I sat by him and held his hand, sending Reiki. Then I felt someone walk up behind me. The air became warmer, and I thought it was either my best friend or my mother. I opened my eyes and turned around only to find no one there. Still, I felt a warm, loving presence behind me, and it grew larger. It seemed to grow to the height of the ceiling, then lean over me until it felt like an enormous cape the length of the bed was surrounding Dad and me. I'd never felt anything like it before. It was very comforting.

After a while, when only a few close family friends remained to keep us company, I turned off the light and whispered in Dad's ear, "It's OK; they're here now." I sat and held his hand until his pulse became slow, then irregular, then a flutter, and then nothing. All the while, the large, warm presence stood over us. I believe deep in my heart that it was an angel behind me, and the "cape" that I felt was wings.

Minutes later, it did not feel like Dad was there any longer. My mom, crying, held his hand. Suddenly, I felt invisible hands on my shoulders, comforting me, and I started to feel tears of comfort welling up. Then Dad's best friend, who had been like a second father to me, came over and put his hands on my shoulders in exactly the same spot as the invisible hands. And that's when my tears broke free.

I am grateful for being able to feel the angelic energies in the room that day and for being open to the loving energy that Reiki provides, so that I could give my father comfort and peace on the last part of his journey home.

About the Contributor

Dawn Wheeler has over fifteen years of experience in health-care marketing and communications. Her interests include holistic medicine, nutrition, and exercise science. She is an Usui Reiki Master and a priest in the Order of Melchizedek. Dawn holds a master's in health science.

"I felt an overwhelming sense of calm and peace fall over me…"

—MARIA BROTTEN, BS, LVT

Finding the Calm Within

BY MARIA BROTTEN, BS, LVT

I STRUGGLED WITH ANXIETY and depression for many years. I've always cared so much about the health and welfare of the special people and animals in my life that oftentimes I'd get caught up in the stress of caring for them and then I'd suffer from anxiety and even periods of depression.

For years, I pursued the traditional treatments of medications and counseling with little effect. Then I began to explore the world of holistic medicine. As a licensed veterinary technician, I saw many animals every day who were also suffering from anxiety and depression.

I felt there had to be better options, not only for myself, but for the companion animals that were often anxious when they came in for treatment at the veterinary hospital.

I decided to attend a local veterinary conference where I heard a wonderful holistic veterinarian lecture on alternative medicine. My pets had previously been treated by her for minor illnesses. At this lecture, she discussed something that was new to me—Reiki. She shared stories of this incredible universal energy and how she was able to bring comfort to sick animals. At that moment, I knew Reiki was something I needed to pursue to enhance my own health as well as the health of the animals I worked with at the hospital.

I signed up for a Reiki training class, though I was unsure of what to expect and I even had doubts that I would be able to give Reiki to myself or to anyone, let alone an animal. My doubts were put to rest when I felt an overwhelming sense of calm and peace fall over me as the class progressed and as I received the Reiki attunement. I left with a sense of purpose in my life. I was here to help others, as well as myself, and Reiki was a new way to do this.

Now, when life gets overwhelming and I'm trying to deal with an issue, I take the time to care for myself. I give myself Reiki or close my eyes and listen to my Reiki chants, and often, a solution will arise. Giving self-Reiki as well as giving Reiki to others is a wonderful experience. Often, my palms become warm as the energy flows through me, and time stands still as I focus on the energy. My intuition takes over, and my hands honestly just go where they are needed and remain at certain spots until I sense it is time to move on. Often, my eyes will close and I'll see shades of colors or other visuals. The whole experience brings extraordinary peace.

Once I learned to dispel my own stress with Reiki, I began to use it for the animals at the veterinary hospital to soothe and comfort them.

Last year, we had a beagle that was dropped off to have some laboratory tests run. It was obvious she was highly anxious. She immediately started digging at the kennel door trying to escape, and she began drooling and panting excessively. I tried comforting her with my words and simple petting, but this had no effect on her. I could see we were both beginning to get frustrated with the situation.

So I decided to try Reiki. I drew several Reiki symbols over her body and told her that I would be there to help her throughout the day. Within a few seconds after I left her, she lay down on her blanket and stopped panting. She was definitely more relaxed than before. Every time I passed her kennel, I thanked her for being such a brave dog and reassured her that the treatments would be done soon and she would be able to go home.

It was a great feeling knowing I had helped this dog deal with her uncontrollable anxiety using nothing more than pure and simple energy and good intention.

Often, I've found that animals are very receptive to the Reiki since they do not overthink the situation. I'm certain that with continued Reiki practice, I will be able to enhance my communication skills with animals.

Sometimes, it is difficult to put myself and my needs first, but I've learned that if I'm not up to par, then I am no use to others in my life. With Reiki, I have learned to find focus on a daily basis to determine what I need to concentrate on at any given time. I don't get frazzled nearly as much as I used to. I'm reminded not to get hung up on the smaller things. Reiki has helped me to see the bigger picture.

Now that I have a child on the way, Reiki has helped me gather the strength and courage needed to help create a calm, loving world for my baby to enter. I am excited to offer Reiki to my child outside the womb, especially during the first few months when my newborn is adjusting to a new life in the world. I believe Reiki will help us bond and communicate with each other through this loving energy.

With Reiki, now I can find peace in my sometimes hectic life, and I'm reminded to take time for myself to relax. This not only helps me and my unborn child but every animal that comes to the hospital for help. Reiki has given me a better understanding of my role on this earth and a renewed feeling of excitement about my future.

About the Contributor

Maria Brotten, BS, LVT is a licensed veterinary technician who has been working with animals for almost ten years. She received her bachelor's degree in veterinary technology to enhance her knowledge in the field. Her special interests include holistic and alternative veterinary medicine and physical rehabilitation. With her Reiki training, Maria is enjoying helping animals at the veterinary clinic and hopes to expand her treatment to local pets in hospice situations.

"I wanted to find a way to have a positive experience with a horse and let go of the fear."

—Yvonne P. Gleason

Horses

BY YVONNE P. GLEASON

I'VE ALWAYS HAD a deep love for animals, and I can't imagine the world without them. I had been giving Reiki to cats and dogs with beneficial results for a long time. I feel especially close to cats and dogs. But there have been several experiences that let me know horses weren't easy for me to feel close to. When I was a child, I had a healthy respect for horses. They were stronger, faster, and bigger than I was. They were also beautiful. So, I signed up to take riding lessons, but in class one day, when the horse didn't follow the teacher's instructions, the teacher admonished the horse. In response, the horse reared up on his hind legs while I was still on his back. Being brand new to riding, I hung on as best as I could. The experience left me feeling a little jittery.

Later, in college, I took a course in training foals. There was a large paddock and stables at one end of the campus. The class went great. I felt it was easy to communicate with the foals, and I became excited about being around horses. Later that year, I made a couple of visits to some of the mares on campus. Neither visit went well. On my first visit, I tried to pet a mare and she bit me. I think my feelings were hurt more than my hand. On the second visit, I was just standing by the fence watching a mare in the paddock and she came over and promptly started eating my hair. I tried to pull it out of her mouth, but of course, that only made her pull the other way even harder. Needless to say, I lost some hair that day.

It was becoming clear: perhaps I just wasn't a "horse person," at least not with *grown* horses. The problem was that my healthy respect for horses was starting to become more of a fear. I knew I had to do something about that.

Going back to a full-grown horse to offer Reiki was a decision that I put some thought into before setting out to do it. I wanted to do it for the benefit of the horse, and I wanted to find a way to have a positive experience with a horse and let go of the fear. I felt that Reiki might be a beginning.

One day, I drove to a park that had horses. Standing near a split-rail fence that enclosed the paddock, I watched a beautiful golden-brown mare in the distance.

I closed my eyes and set the intention for the highest and best for the mare. I created a Reiki space around me full of light and unconditional love from Source. I felt very relaxed as I allowed my palms to open and let the Reiki flow from my hands. I stayed like that for a few moments.

With my eyes still closed, I heard the thud-thud of hooves come closer and closer, and then it stopped. I opened my eyes to find the mare right in front of me, just one foot away.

That's when I noticed a red gash in her right side, which was directly across from my open hands. The wound looked like it had been doctored with some salve. I had no doubt that she had consciously positioned herself so that her wound was across from the Reiki flowing from my hands. I held my position and took a deep, relaxing breath, continuing to allow the Reiki to flow.

The mare held her position too. Then she closed her eyes. After a couple of moments, she leaned her whole body toward my hands. With her eyes still closed, she began to sway from side to side as if she were starting to fall asleep. I continued to let the Reiki flow through me to her.

After the session, she remained calm. I thanked her silently. And I thanked Higher Power for the opportunity to be of help.

Then a handler came for her, and I watched as she was led away toward the stable.

To see such a large and powerful animal react so quickly to the Reiki was a wonderful experience for me. At last, I had experienced a positive interaction with a full-grown horse, thanks to the Reiki.

I now understand another aspect of horses, and I have a new appreciation for them. Often, I think of my "Reiki mare," and I smile and send her love.

"I was becoming aware of the 'spirit' of plants in a way I had never experienced before."

—GEORGEANN CASEY

A Reiki Awakening

BY GEORGEANN CASEY

I DECIDED TO PURSUE Reiki training so that I could use it as a healing modality, not only to help myself, but to help my family and friends.

I have worked with plants as a landscape designer for twenty-five years. What I didn't expect was that after completing my Reiki training, my soul would be awakened to a completely different aspect of plants.

I had worked with only the ornamental aspect of plants, designing landscapes. Then Reiki gently awakened something in me, and I began considering the medicinal and healing value of plants. I was becoming aware of the "spirit" of plants in a way I had never experienced before.

As my interest grew, I decided to move to North Carolina to pursue herbal medicine. The move to a different state could have been a nerve-wracking experience, but during the whole process of the move, I felt the support of the universe through Reiki; the transition was smooth.

I feel Reiki has led me to my true calling after all these years. I've begun to realize that plants have so much to give us—not only their outer beauty but their inner beauty. I'm amazed to find how much their medicinal properties have the ability to help us heal physically and spiritually. I combine the use of plants with Reiki to help myself and my loved ones.

To me, the most profound thing about Reiki is that I did not feel I had to be special or be a "healer" to heal. I could just do it. I have to say the results have been remarkable. I can heal the smallest cut to larger issues, and it has been very empowering to take control of my own healing on both a physical and spiritual level.

Reiki changed my life and is continuing to expand it every day. I only wish I had not waited so long to find it.

About the Contributor

Georgeann Casey, a landscape designer for twenty-five years, lives in North Carolina and works with plants and their healing properties. She is happy to give Reiki to friends and family members whenever needed.

"To my surprise, no one was at my ankles or anywhere near my feet, yet I felt a tall energetic presence and loving hands."

—LORRAINE WALKER, PHD

All I Have to Do Is Ask

BY LORRAINE WALKER, PʜD

A S I WAS DRIVING to a Reiki share one evening, I was feeling tired, achy, and cranky. I was dealing with a restless leg that caused a lot of discomfort and distress, particularly in the evening hours. On the way to the share, I drove past the cemetery where my brother is buried. He died after a courageous struggle with multiple myeloma just one year earlier.

It is not uncommon for me to drive by this cemetery and send a blessing his way believing that, on some level, he receives it. On this particular evening, I drove by and called to him. He was always a very generous person, and feeling a little bit in need, I asked him for a return blessing. Not thinking anything more about it, I drove on to the share.

As I lay on the Reiki table, I could feel the Reiki energy pulsing through my body. It was strong and had a very loving quality to it. As my practitioner slowly moved down my body from my head to my feet, the energy intensified. I could feel it traveling rapidly up from my feet through my legs and torso to my head. The next thing I remember was hearing my practitioner say a closing prayer. I thought, *That's odd. How can the session be over when my practitioner is still working at my feet?* In fact, I could even feel the presence of his strong hands on my ankles. Then, I felt a tap on my shoulder to notify me once again that the session had ended. Completely perplexed, I opened my eyes only to see my practitioner standing by my shoulder. To my surprise, no one was at my ankles or anywhere near my feet, yet I felt a tall, energetic presence and loving hands.

I didn't tell anyone about this. For a moment, I thought maybe I'd fallen asleep and the energy I had sensed was part of a dream. Then, what I had been feeling was validated. One of the intuitive practitioners said that the energetic presence of a "tall gentleman" had been working on my feet next to my practitioner.

Immediately, I knew in my heart that the "tall gentleman" was my brother. I was surprised and pleased. I whispered, "Thank you," to my brother. He had come to give me a blessing as I had requested. It was a confirmation of an old adage: "Ask and you will receive." I had asked, and in return, I was shown the power of love and connection beyond the physical world, as our loved ones reach out to us across time and space.

About the Contributor

Lorraine Walker, PhD, is a Reiki Master who uses her intuition, insight, and inquiry skills to assist others in their journey to wholeness. She is also an educator and a professional life coach who uses her Reiki skills to promote well-being in body, mind, and spirit. She is a member of the International Association for Reiki Training, the International Coach Federation, and Edgar Cayce's Association for Research and Enlightenment. She can be reached at lwalker8@gmail.com.

"This is part of who I am..."

—Diane Foster

On the Path
to Helping Others

BY DIANE FOSTER

I T WAS MY LITTLE NIECE who inspired me to begin my quest to learn a healing energy modality. She was born with physical challenges, and she experienced pain daily. She had difficulty swallowing, eating, walking, sleeping, under-standing—you name it. I felt very helpless. I was here in the United States, and she was in France. Yet I wanted to help, even from a distance. I began to think about distance healing to help stop her pain and help her to thrive.

I thought of the power of faith, where people just lay hands upon others. I was inspired by the stories of Jesus, Father Pio, and those whose faith healed others, and I remembered Jesus said something to the effect that whatever he did, any of us could do. I felt myself drawn to energy healing.

A family member, due to her beliefs, urged me not to take any energy modality courses, but the calling within me grew stronger. I didn't want to upset my family, and I was afraid if I took the courses that I would be restricted from seeing my niece. But the calling grew even stronger, and after some hesitation, I eventually signed up for an energy healing course. This soon was followed by a Reiki training course.

Now I'm grateful I heeded the call. Whenever I'm "in healing energy mode," I feel a strong and beautiful connection to God's love and light. Since taking my Reiki class, I've used Reiki for many situations.

One of those situations took place about eight years ago. My relatives arrived from France for the Christmas holidays, and the next morning, my great-aunt, age ninety-four, fell and broke her hip.

I stayed with my aunt from the ambulance to the hospital so I could translate for her what the medical personnel were asking. Right after my aunt came out of surgery and while she was still asleep in the ICU, I asked the nurses if I could see her. I was authorized just a five-minute visit, since many other patients close by were also recovering.

I approached her bedside and just started doing "my thing," giving the energy. I felt the ICU nurses' curious glances from a distance. Within the next five minutes, the nurse assigned to my great-aunt came by to tell me that time was up, so I stopped.

However, as she spoke, she also took note of the monitors tracking my great-aunt's vital signs. She seemed surprised; she turned to me and said, "That's OK. You can stay as long as you want. Whatever you are doing, keep doing it." Then she left.

I was permitted to stay for the next hour, until my great-aunt woke up.

Reiki has provided me with the opportunity to delve further into the world of subtle energies. I have been able to develop my awareness more via "feeling" versus "seeing." The ability to open up intuitively has helped me grow tremendously spiritually.

Whenever I see someone who may need some healing energy, I offer it gladly—sometimes overtly, sometimes not. I'm grateful I followed the calling. Now I know that this is part of who I am and it is something I can offer my little niece and others in the world.

About the Contributor

Diane Foster is a program manager by day with a company providing engineering services for the government. She leads a diverse team of systems and aviation engineers, regularly meets with a sensitives support group during the week, and loves to swing dance on weekends. As opportunities arise, she offers healing energy treatments to friends, family, and pets.

"… when I noticed that my beloved cat, Midnight, wasn't well, I decided to see if distance Reiki could help him."

—STEPHANIE PHILLIPS

Distance Reiki for My Cats

BY STEPHANIE PHILLIPS

I HAD BEEN IN PAIN for a long time after I'd had a car accident. Finally, I received a Reiki treatment, and when I left the session, the pain was greatly reduced. So, when I noticed that one of my beloved cats, Midnight, wasn't well, I wondered if distance Reiki could help him. After all, if Reiki had helped me, maybe it would help my cat too.

My other cat, Princess Ivy, had been acting OK, her usual aloof self. But Midnight had been licking himself so much that he was missing fur in spots all over his body. Clearly, I needed to find out what was wrong.

So I scheduled a distance Reiki session for him. The practitioner had never seen either of my cats before. She gave distance

Reiki from her Reiki studio in another city from the one I lived in. I knew the day and time she was going to give the Reiki. I arranged to be in a quiet, loving space at the same time she was sending the Reiki. I was told this wasn't necessary for the Reiki to be effective, but I wanted to have a calm and quiet time with Midnight while the Reiki was being sent to him.

After the session, the practitioner said that the energy around Midnight's stomach felt blocked. I needed to take him to the vet anyway, so once I was at the vet I asked to have his stomach checked out just in case something was up. It turned out that Midnight had worms in his intestines!

The practitioner also said that during the distance session, she sensed that the emotional field of Princess Ivy was unbalanced. I then had to admit that I'd always favored Midnight because he was "my" cat and Princess Ivy was my son's cat.

I have since made a point to give equal affection to both cats. Midnight went on medicine to get rid of the worms. Midnight is doing great, and whenever I have a Reiki session in my home, Princess Ivy sits very closely and purrs quite loudly. All is well with the cats in our house now.

The Reiki went right where it needed to go for my cats and even gave me information about my cats that allowed me to further help them.

It's true that what's good for me, is also good for my cats. Now we are one big, happy Reiki family!

About the Contributor

Stephanie Phillips is a thirty-one-year-old mother of one. She is the manager of Project Services during the day and a partner in Eden's Balance, a natural skin-care company. She can be reached at stephanie@edensbalance.com.

"My friend was now on the final peaceful leg of her journey."

—JASMIN EL KORDI

Preparing the Way
for My Friend

BY JASMIN EL KORDI

I HAD THE GREAT FORTUNE to give Reiki treatments to my dear friend during the last part of her life's journey. She was a successful professional in the mental health field and was accomplished in all aspects of her life. She was an experienced meditator, and she worked to consciously expand her connection to Source.

She was as committed to her soul-growth as she was to her professional life, and in the process, she brought out the best in everyone who knew her. She definitely brought out the best in me.

One day early on in our weekly Reiki treatment sessions, we spent some time putting context and meaning around each step of her journey, her relationships, and all that she had created in her life. During our conversation, she suddenly looked at me and said, "I think you are my spiritual teacher." I felt awestruck. I was honored to be considered her teacher for her spiritual growth.

I began to learn more deeply that all I had to do was let the Reiki flow in order to help "teach" my friend what she needed to know at that moment. The Reiki brought us the gift of lessons, and as I gave Reiki to her throughout the following months, there were many lessons for her—and for me, which rose to the surface during the sessions. I was just grateful to be a part of the process.

Then one day, after her Reiki session, we came to a plateau in the journey, and she turned to me with tears in her eyes and said, "I have finally learned to love unconditionally."

Again, I was awestruck. "That is all we are really meant to do," I said.

Then she added, "I know it will be all right."

I left that afternoon with the knowledge that my friend was now on the final peaceful leg of her journey.

When I saw her one last time, as I brushed my hands slowly over her aura, I found her energy system to be completely balanced and extremely vibrant.

When the time came and she passed peacefully, she had already become serenely connected to Source. Reiki allowed me to be a messenger of love and support from the universe and a guide for her spiritual growth during the last part of her life's journey.

Now, whenever I think of my friend, I feel her light, and I know everything is all right.

About the Contributor

Jasmin El Kordi is a national sales manager for Cisco and is passionate about facilitating transformation for those whose lives she touches. Reiki is an important aspect of her life, and it is a modality through which she guides and helps others. She can be reached at jasminel-kordi@hotmail.com.

"It seemed they were helping me with the healing session."

—Hildegard B. Groves, RMP Usui Reiki,
Karuna Reiki®

A Welcome Visit

BY HILDEGARD B. GROVES,
RMP USUI REIKI, KARUNA REIKI®

MY COUSIN AND I were on vacation in a cottage built on a tiny peninsula nestled within three hundred acres of wetlands near the Chesapeake Bay. This is one of the most peaceful places I have ever encountered and very conducive to the relaxing practice of Reiki. The marshland and meandering canals teem with shorebirds foraging for food. The sunrises and sunsets are stupendous.

It was here that I had a very spiritual experience while giving a Reiki session to my cousin.

As I allowed the energy to flow, I proceeded to give Reiki to my cousin's upper body. Then I glanced down to the end of the table, and I saw a surprising sight. There, working on her feet, were her parents who had both passed years before!

It seemed they were helping me with the healing session. They never looked up at me, nor did they appear to notice me.

We continued to give Reiki together, and then at some point, her parents disappeared.

After the session, I told my cousin about them. She was not surprised at their presence, and we were both fascinated by their "visit."

I feel they were there that day because they knew their daughter needed their additional assistance.

There have been a few other instances during Reiki sessions when I have been aware of entities assisting me, usually clients' relatives.

As a Reiki practitioner, I've learned that I am available as a channel through which healing energy flows. After years of practicing, it is still such a privilege and an honor to practice this beautiful energy work for those who are drawn to me, and it is so special to attract their loved ones during the sessions to enhance the healing.

About the Contributor

Hildegard B. Groves is a Master Practitioner of Usui Reiki and Karuna Reiki®. Her office is located in Gaithersburg, Maryland. She can be reached at hbgroves@gmail.com.

"If I want to improve the world, I have to start by improving upon and loving myself."

—JEFFREY FRIEDMAN

A Path to Loving
and Healing Myself

BY JEFFREY FRIEDMAN

AFTER YEARS of being drawn to the healing arts, I decided to pursue Reiki training, and in 2003, I became a Reiki Master.

Through Reiki, I've learned that if I want to improve the world, I have to start by improving upon and loving myself. I need to continue to work on myself, physically, emotionally, mentally, and spiritually in order to evolve.

Receiving distance Reiki, while giving self-Reiki, has been very effective in healing my physical ailments and has helped me through challenging times.

Not long ago, I had the hiccups for more than two weeks. It might sound funny, but it's not funny when you have them all the time. And I had them all the time. It was exhausting and hard to sleep. Nobody knew why I had the hiccups. I knew the hiccups disappeared whenever I performed self-Reiki with meditation. But then right after my session, the hiccups would return. I knew there was a lesson I needed to learn, and I set out to find it. I needed to stop the hiccups once and for all. Meditation didn't give me the answer. My spiritual teacher couldn't give me the answer.

Finally, my Reiki instructor sent me distance Reiki, and that worked. That energy was what eventually made the hiccups stop. With my Reiki instructor's intuition, he helped me realize the root cause of the hiccups: I was feeling overwhelmed at work. I had been doing a lot of the work myself. My Reiki instructor helped me to set a new intention. I knew I needed to hire more staff for my business. When I set that as my intention, then the hiccups started to go away. During that time, I had been giving myself Reiki as well. So, the combination of the distance Reiki, setting a new intention, and self-Reiki all helped my body return to a state of relaxation. The hiccups left me, and I had a new task: to restructure my work environment for the better.

This wasn't the first time that I have been healed through Reiki. At one time, I had a huge lump under my left arm. It had been there for two years. Again, I had a session receiving distance Reiki while simultaneously giving self-Reiki to that area of my body. Two days later, the lump disappeared.

Reiki has helped me with healing many things in my body, my mind, and my soul and has helped me to love myself unconditionally.

One way I improve upon loving myself unconditionally is by giving Reiki to myself on a daily basis. Often, I combine meditation with self-Reiki. I put one hand on my heart chakra and one hand on my solar plexus. It balances out the energy and heals my whole body. I feel energy moving up my legs and going into all parts of my body. Sometimes I see pictures and see or hear messages, but usually, they are on a very deep level. Often, I'm aware that I'm being given information, but I usually don't consciously know what it is. I trust the process and know I'm learning on a subconscious level all that I need to know to help me grow spiritually.

Reiki has served as a constant reminder to me that we are not human beings having spiritual experiences; we are spiritual beings having human experiences.

I feel blessed to have the opportunity to offer my gifts to help others and to serve those individuals that God sends my way each day.

About the Contributor

Jeffrey Friedman is a Reiki Master and the president of Pro Lawns Complete Landscape, Inc. He hosts monthly Reiki healing circles in Maryland. For more information, go to: http://www.reikihealingcircle.org.

"The greatest surprise was the desire I began to feel to help others with Reiki."

—LINDSAY S. WEGERT

Magnolia Bloom

BY LINDSAY S. WEGERT

AS A CHILD, I was very intuitive. I seemed to just "know" things about people, and many spirits and angel friends came to visit me. Very early on, I started to become aware of my own consciousness and my connection to all living things. It wasn't until later that Reiki would come into my life and propel me into much deeper growth.

I had a significant experience when I was very small, while sitting in the kitchen sink amid the warm, sudsy water of my bath. Just outside the window there was a brilliant object that was being guided to and fro by an invisible force. This object, a huge magnolia bloom, vibrated in the sunlight. My breath partnered with the gentle invisible force that played with the magnolia bloom. I was "at one" with the breeze, the bloom, the light. The bouquet filled the center of my being, and my eyes closed. Streams of water trickled down my face. The fragrance danced with an almost uncontainable feeling of joy. Joy was my whole being. I realized that I was alive. "Alive" meant energy vibrations and sensing beauty around me. "Alive" meant being in the unconditional love. I knew I could be a part of moments like these and I could take part in creating them. I *was* that love.

As I grew, I experienced more of these "being alive" moments. My intuition also grew, coaxed by the loving energies of Mother Earth, my helper spirits, and the elementals.

As an adult, I sought out Reiki training for my own healing and growth. The right teacher was there at the right time with the right lessons.

I was surprised to find that Reiki played a large part in the further development of my intuition. Suddenly, I was able to sense the energy of others more easily and more frequently. But the greatest surprise was the desire I began to feel to help others with Reiki.

Eventually, I followed that desire and I began to give Reiki to others, combining the energy work of Reiki with my developing intuitive awareness.

I started volunteering to give Reiki to cancer patients at the Life with Cancer Family Center. I've been there for six years now. In my Reiki treatment sessions, my intuition lets me know where to give the Reiki and I'm always assisted by my Reiki guides and my familiar childhood elementals.

I've been fortunate to bring the gift of Reiki into my home life, to others who need healing energy, and to my professional world.

Like the magnolia bloom of my childhood, my intuitive growth has blossomed. Reiki continues to be a part of my ongoing growth, and it allows me to be a part of helping others to grow into their greatest potential.

About the Contributor

Lindsay S. Wegert has been a Virginia licensed optician for over thirty years. Her intuitive skills combined with her work with Reiki help her to know and understand her customers' needs even before they tell her. She holds a small Reiki practice.

"We had a lot of power outages. Everything just went down all at once.... But this time, I just knew intuitively what the issue was."

—TIM GLEASON

My Path to Better Job Performance

BY TIM GLEASON

A T MY JOB, I just drifted along with the current. Often, I'd get overwhelmed with tasks. It was hard for me to prioritize and focus. I felt stuck. I was tired of feeling like I was always on a treadmill just going around and around.

Then I began to receive regular Reiki treatments. Over time, the Reiki helped improve my ability to focus on my tasks at work. Now I can get to a place where I can block out all the peripheral noise and just sit there and do what I need to do. With regular Reiki sessions, I know this will improve even more over time. Being able to focus has helped me to be more efficient at work.

But the biggest improvement I received from Reiki was the strengthening of my intuition, which has helped with my troubleshooting skills. Before Reiki, I looked at everything from a technical perspective, and I didn't have a strong intuitive knowledge of how to solve problems that came up on the job. Problem-solving is so much easier now that I can use both my intuition and my technical knowledge. It has helped me numerous times.

There was a particular day at work when I needed all the brain power I could summon up. We had a lot of power outages. Everything just went down all at once.

Usually, this situation indicates that someone in the network is causing the problem. But this time, I just knew intuitively what the issue was. I saw a picture of it in my head. It was a power supply problem in the data center. And guess what? That turned out to be the exact issue. I made one phone call, and my theory was verified. It turned out someone had done a power test and it had shut everything off. My intuitive solution saved a lot of time.

Last year, I went to a job interview, and I was able to say that one of my biggest strengths is being able to see things from the next level up and that I intuitively understand how things interact. When I see a problem with a particular set of symptoms, I usually know how to find the solution. I wouldn't have been able to say that about myself before.

Now I can perform efficiently at work, no matter what job I find myself in. I'm able to use my intuition to help myself and my coworkers find solutions to whatever problem might arise.

Reiki has increased my self-confidence, and this has allowed me to take on more complicated tasks. Finally, I'm taking steps forward at work. I'm no longer stuck. I'm moving ahead, and I have Reiki to thank for that.

About the Contributor

Tim Gleason enjoys working with computers. When he isn't working, he can be found in the mountains or on the beach. He can be reached at waninick@verizon.net.

"I could feel the energy moving through my physical body and energy bodies."

—STEPHANIE PHILLIPS

Opening Up to Love

BY STEPHANIE PHILLIPS

I BEGAN A SPIRITUAL JOURNEY in 2008 after my mother died from ovarian cancer, only a month before her forty-seventh birthday. For the first time in my life, I was completely lost. I didn't just lose my mother; it was as though I had lost my sister and best friend as well. I felt like I was drowning in a sea of people, screaming for help, but no sound would come out and no one could hear my pleas.

Luckily, divine timing is never late; people started coming into my life, at first, in what seemed to be random coincidences. These new friends helped me to heal. I started reading books on positivity and spirituality. I began my yoga practice again and was anticipating an upcoming month-long Integral Yoga teacher training. I wrote in my gratitude journal every day, my bedroom walls were scattered with dream boards, and I tried to be the most positive Stephanie I could be.

Then almost a year after mom transitioned, I was in a car accident. Although it seemed like minor damage at first, I had chronic pain in my neck, back, knee, and ankle. After months of physical therapy and discussing surgery with my doctors, I knew that I had to try something different. I knew that energy work was what I needed. I decided to try Reiki.

My first experience with Reiki was profound. During my Reiki session, I could feel the energy moving through my physical body and energy bodies. The most interesting part was all of the sensations I felt—cool, warm, hot, and tingly—and my practitioner's hands weren't even touching my physical body most of the time. The session cleared a lot of emotional and physical pain that I had carried for a while. I walked out of my treatment session with my pain levels drastically reduced.

After the session, all I could think about was how this modality of healing could benefit people and I felt a deep urgency inside of me that I could not suppress. I wanted to learn how to do this. I signed up for a Reiki training class.

During my Reiki class, we practiced giving and receiving the Reiki. As I was lying on the table, receiving Reiki, suddenly, I felt the presence of my mother so strongly that I burst into tears of happiness. I knew my mother was right there. Only seconds later, my Reiki teacher shared with me that she felt a loving female presence standing next to me. It was a confirmation for me that I was on the right path for my highest good.

Since that Reiki experience, I know more deeply that my mother is never far away. From time to time, I feel her presence, and I smile, knowing she is with me.

Reiki has helped me open up to love; self-love, love for humanity, and love for all that is. Today, I'm very grateful for where I am on my spiritual path, and Reiki has been an amazing tool along the way.

About the Contributor

This is Stephanie Phillips's second story for *Reiki Journeys.* Her bio appears on page 49.

"Sarah left earth, looking as beautiful as ever."

—G. Mary Walton

Simba and Sarah

BY G. MARY WALTON

IN 2007, with the help of Spirit and my dear friend, I was
guided down a path toward Reiki. Since then, I've found
that Reiki is a path of intuitive and spiritual growth.

I've had quite a few intuitive visions and dreams since working with Reiki, but one of the most memorable ones was the
vision I received on January 8, 2012. This vision involved two
cat faces and a bear face. One cat was black, and the other cat
had white around its nose.

I knew the black cat represented my cat, Simba. Simba was
an outdoor cat, and I was blessed to have him come indoors for
some "petting time" every now and then, in between his daily
adventures outside.

In the vision, the cat with the white around her nose was my
cat, Sarah.

The very next day after the vision, I took Simba to the veterinarian to be neutered. When Simba was placed under for surgery, it was discovered that he had heartworms and feline AIDS. I had to put my dear Simba to sleep.

After he passed, I was left with five other cats, but Sarah and I had developed a very close bond throughout the years. Of all six cats, only Sarah appeared to be interested in the Reiki energy. Whenever I had certain Reiki clients on the table, Sarah would come into the room and want to join the client on the table. I nicknamed Sarah "my little Reiki girl." Sarah received numerous Reiki treatments, and I think she gave Reiki to others as well. I now believe Sarah was a healer.

Just eleven days after I'd had the vision, Sarah fell ill and was diagnosed with kidney disease. I gave her Reiki every day. The veterinarians were amazed when they discovered her kidney levels were so high and yet Sarah was still eating.

Then the time came, and Sarah told me she was ready to leave this earth plane and go to Rainbow Bridge. She had stopped eating completely. The veterinarian was very surprised to see how well Sarah looked and that she was not skinny at all.

In February, Sarah left earth, looking as beautiful as ever. I firmly believe the Reiki gave Sarah more time on earth and a better quality of life.

I've since read that a bear's kidneys shut down in winter when they hibernate. I thought about the bear's face in the vision that I'd received in early January. My friend said that Sarah was probably sending a message, letting me know that she was going to pass soon with kidney failure.

Since leaving her physical body, Sarah has contacted me and has sent lots of love. I still miss her, but I've received so many signs from her. Sarah was, and still is, a great inspiration to me.

Though Simba and Sarah have transitioned, with Reiki in my life, I do not feel alone.

My relationship with Reiki teaches me something new and extraordinary with each passing year.

I have angels, spirit guides, and many helpers from the spiritual realm near me always, helping to prepare me for what's to come, through visions and dreams. I feel there is a "cushion of love" around me and in me.

About the Contributor

G. Mary Walton is a Karuna Reiki® Master who lives in Northeast Ohio. She shares her semirural home with cats Petey, Nate, Tessa, Emma, Fluffy, and the beautiful spirit of Sarah. She continues an amazing spiritual journey with her angels and spirit guides of light and love. She can be reached at smokyretreat@frontier.com.

"I learned that my sensitive nature was something to feel good about, not something to be ashamed of."

—LYNN SCULLEN

My Journey to an All-Embracing Universe

BY LYNN SCULLEN

WHEN I WAS A LITTLE GIRL, I could sense the energy of other people, and I would feel it intensely. Whenever I met someone, I could sense if he or she wasn't looking out for my best interests. The problem was that sometimes what I sensed was so strong that I would become cautious or fearful or begin to cry. I was labeled as "oversensitive." Sometimes I'd get overwhelmed and lose my sense of my own energy, and then I might faint.

I was raised in a strict Catholic family, and I had been told not to question anything about our religion. But as I grew into a teenager, I wondered why God would give me a questioning brain if I wasn't supposed to use it. I had a lot of questions:

"Does God care what we wear in church?" "Is God only in church or is God everywhere?" I wanted to connect to Source, but I had trouble making a connection that felt right for me.

I had a best friend who was Jewish. My mom told me that my best friend would not be going to heaven and that only *I* would go, if I continued my Catholic practices. I didn't understand. Why would God leave my friend behind? If my best friend wasn't going to heaven, I didn't want to go either.

Later, when I went away to college, I was encouraged to question and think for myself. It was during that year that my mother unexpectedly passed away. My mom had been a good Catholic, and yet she had died. Again, I asked, "Why?"

I began to search for something to believe in that resonated more with my way of thinking. That's when I found Reiki.

I signed up for a Reiki class with my sister. It felt like I was coming home to myself. In that class, I learned that my sensitive nature was something to feel good about, not something to be ashamed of. I was amazed to learn about the concept of an energy field around the body and the idea that we can balance the energies to promote health and healing. My Reiki teacher helped me to appreciate my ability to sense others' energies. I learned that sensing the quality of energy in the fields and chakras of another person can be helpful when giving Reiki to him or her.

Reiki provided ways for me to center and ground my energy. I learned that my ability to feel the energy could be controlled so that I would not be prone to sadness or fainting spells whenever the energy I sensed was very strong.

Reiki gave me a new way to perceive what I knew in my heart to be true about myself. I had to unlearn the negative childhood associations with being sensitive and open up to a different way of thinking. I welcomed this as a growth opportunity.

Reiki helped me to know more fully that the universe provides when we are in need. It provides for all of us and embraces every one of us, including my best friend from childhood.

I'm grateful to find others like myself who share this same way of thinking.

Reiki continues to help me open the door to new discoveries and friendships, and it satisfies my deep childhood longing for a way to connect with Spirit.

About the Contributor

Lynn Scullen has a master's degree in social work. She is an early childhood specialist, and she loves to give Reiki to her family and friends.

"I knew that if the Reiki didn't help in a matter of seconds, we'd be heading for the clinic."

—Yvonne P. Gleason

Reiki for My Cat

BY YVONNE P. GLEASON

I HAD READ THAT REIKI can be very beneficial for animals but it wasn't until I adopted my cat, Wani, that I found out first-hand just how effective Reiki can be for our beloved animal friends.

Wani had a gentle disposition and an affinity for being on my lap. He was my soul-cat. As the years passed, our bond deepened. He and I went through several moves as my job changed from one location to another, and eventually, I met and married a man whom Wani and I both loved.

It wasn't long before my husband and I found out that Wani had an issue with his bowels that caused inflammation, and sometimes Wani would suffer from constipation. He'd strain to go in his litter box, but often it was without success. This would happen usually around 2:00 a.m. on a week night, and we'd have to take him to the emergency clinic, which was in another city. Not a fun trip for any of us.

Usually, an enema was the protocol, and it wasn't well tolerated by Wani. It left him listless for days afterward. A low dose of prednisone was prescribed, although we'd been warned of possible side effects.

I had nothing to lose when one night, as Wani was just beginning to have one of his straining episodes, I decided to try to give him some Reiki. Doing this proved much more difficult than I had thought. It was so hard seeing my Wani so uncomfortable. It took everything I had to just calm myself down and trust the process of Reiki, as I had been taught.

I closed my eyes, took a deep breath, and although Wani was visibly uncomfortable, I placed one hand over his stomach and the other hand over his backside and I let the Reiki flow. I knew that if the Reiki didn't help in a matter of seconds, we'd be heading for the clinic. I didn't want to prolong his discomfort. I glanced at my watch and made note of the time.

Then something amazing happened. Wani stopped straining. It was almost immediate. I continued to give the Reiki a moment longer. Then I ended the session. Wani was quiet as he walked over to the litter box and . . . success!

Then he walked out of the litter box, curled up on his favorite pillow, and promptly fell asleep.

I was overjoyed.

So, this became the first protocol I took with Wani whenever the constipation episodes started. I learned to remain calm and give the Reiki a chance. Our late-hour drives to the emergency clinic became very few indeed.

Whenever Wani had discomfort in his stomach, he would come over to me, and press his stomach against my hands. It helped him greatly.

Wani had trusted me to help him. All I'd had to do was trust the Reiki.

"I began to actually feel her hands on top of mine."
—Susan L. Bajnoczy, MSW, RN, CNOR

A Visit from a
Special Reiki Guide

BY SUSAN L. BAJNOCZY,
MSW, RN, CNOR

REIKI CAME TO ME while I was researching complementary and alternative medicine (CAM) as I was completing my graduate degree in nursing. I was interested in a modality that would treat the cause of a patient's disease, not just the symptoms.

I admit at first I was a bit skeptical about Reiki, but I wanted to see for myself what it was all about. Eventually, I received a Reiki treatment, and then I began to study Reiki. In my Reiki classes, the instructor taught us to call upon Reiki guides for assistance. Right away, my "inner skeptic" came to the forefront. There were Reiki guides who could help us? I wasn't so sure about that.

Then I experienced something that helped me to validate and trust in the process, and my skepticism began to fade.

Shortly after I received my attunement, during a meditation, I began to sense very strongly the energies of Sensei Usui, Doctor Hayashi, and Mrs. Takata, the founders of Reiki. My Reiki guides and ancestors were becoming known to me. I could see their faces very clearly. I experienced Sensei Usui as a very loving and compassionate energy. I felt his expansive joy and an incredible sense of humor. For me, Dr. Hayashi's energy was extremely gentle and compassionate. I experienced Mrs. Takata's energy as firm and strict.

Then something happened to further validate the process. While I was providing a Reiki treatment, Mrs. Takata clearly appeared. I began to actually feel her hands on top of mine. At first, I did not completely welcome her arrival. She seemed so firm. But when she placed her hands upon mine, my hands got extremely hot—so hot that the person receiving the treatment actually commented on it. This continued to happen whenever I gave treatment sessions.

When I was participating in a Reiki share, once again, Mrs. Takata appeared and placed her hands on mine, and the person receiving energy aroused from a relaxed state and wondered whose hands were so hot!

Through my experiences, I've come to understand Mrs. Takata's energy to be that of great compassion and dedication.

Mrs. Takata continues to drop in occasionally, but instead of placing her hands over mine, she stands by to make sure that I am performing Reiki with correct hand placement. She seems satisfied with my progress.

I understand the concept that time is a continuum and Reiki energy can be transmitted to the past, present, and future. This helps me to realize how it is possible for me to have these experiences with Mrs. Takata's energy.

Even now, as a Usui-Tibetan and Karuna Reiki® Master, sometimes my "inner skeptic" returns and causes me to question whether the energy will work this time, if it will be strong enough, or if the attunements that I give will really take.

Then I think of Mrs. Takata and our many Reiki ancestors and guides who are here to help us develop our skills in the effort to help ourselves and others.

Reiki has opened my heart on a spiritual level, which has helped me to express gratitude for each and every sensei, whether on the physical plane or in another dimension.

Reiki has become so much a part of my daily life, it is like breathing, and it has helped me to fulfill my mission to help others. I believe this treatment modality is on its way to becoming well integrated into the Western medical paradigm.

About the Contributor

Susan L. Bajnoczy, MSW, RN, CNOR, currently works as a nurse and educator at an intercity trauma, teaching, and research hospital in Richmond. Her interest in energy medicine began as a novice nurse over twenty years ago when a Healing Touch (HT) practitioner trained volunteer nurses as Level I HT practitioners. This energy modality has been utilized as a nursing intervention and is now effectively integrated into Western medicine, resulting in holistic care. Encouraged by this, Susan continued to study energy medicine and the ways it can enhance mainstream contemporary health care.

Now she is a Reiki Master/Teacher who provides classes to health-care workers in an effort to pay forward the benefits of the loving Reiki energy to others. She resides in Virginia with her husband, teenage son, and two beautiful English bulldogs who are frequent recipients of Reiki.

"I knew what I was called to do in this lifetime."

—Briana Isenhart

Opening Doors

BY BRIANA ISENHART

I RECEIVED MY REIKI TRAINING from a very special person... my mom.

During my Reiki Second Degree attunement, I had a vision that helped lead me to where I am today. As I sat in my chair, letting the music consume me, I began to drift away as I envisioned myself as a Native American girl. I knew this was a special farewell ceremony for me, but I didn't know where I was going. Then I saw an old, wise man approach me. He wore a feathered headdress that went down to the floor. As he looked into my eyes, I knew he was the chief of the tribe. I had a feeling that our connection together was deep. When I asked him who he was, he replied, "I'm your father." He placed a necklace around my neck. It was made of animal bones, and it had a small bottle in the center.

My grandmother stood next to him holding a wooden box. Inside was a bow and arrow. My father said, "You have a mission to follow the eagle to where he flies. The bow and arrow are for protection." Then he and my grandmother led me over to the tepee. We went inside, and I took a seat. I bowed my head as my father held my hands, and I began to cry as he gave me the gift of healing. My body began heating up from the inside out; it was the most powerful experience of my life.

Then I met a wolf who would stay by my side. We began walking through the woods, and through the breaks in the treetops, I saw the bald eagle that I would be following on my journey to different tribes to heal people.

After the attunement, I knew what I was called to do in this lifetime. I embarked on a journey of healing and teaching others this natural modality of loving energy from Source.

I began working for a hospice facility. I found that Reiki automatically starts flowing through my hands when I'm visiting patients. When I'm sitting with patients who are at the end of life and they're experiencing pain, sadness, or fear, my hands become extremely hot and it lasts the duration of the visit.

Sometimes I even feel a warm sensation that starts from my solar plexus and flows throughout my entire body. For me, this is a sign that the patients need some support. So I will take a moment to say a prayer for the loving, healing energy to surround them and bring them comfort before sending Reiki. Sometimes I will see a physical change in their behavior. They may smile or seem more relaxed. But most of the time, I believe that Reiki goes to them on a deeper level, a subconscious and spiritual level.

I know the Reiki will always go where it is needed. That's the neat thing about Reiki—I don't have to direct it to go any particular place. I've learned that Reiki is activated by intention—my intention for Source to heal in a way that's right for each individual.

Reiki is very helpful in my everyday life as well. It has opened a whole new door for me by helping me to develop my intuitive capabilities. This has allowed me to become more aware of the energies of others so that I can have the opportunity to help them, and it has taught me to listen to my inner guidance.

With Reiki, I can send distance healing to my family, raise the vibrations of my home, or send positive energy to any situation, and the Reiki truly works.

Reiki has shaped the person I am today. Now I try to bring a positive, all-loving energy wherever I go and to whomever I meet, and I set the intention to be a clear channel for God's healing energy to flow through me to anyone who needs it. I feel blessed to be a part of this process.

About the Contributor

Briana Isenhart works as a business manager for a local hospice. She is a Reiki Master/ Teacher and has been practicing for four years. She has volunteered giving Reiki to oncology patients and loves giving Reiki to friends and family. She enjoys educating others on how to heal holistically using God's loving energy. She can be reached at briana.isenhart@gmail.com.

"I was breathing, but I wasn't living. What could I do?"

—Lindsay Curtis

Finding My Life Purpose

BY LINDSAY CURTIS

LIKE MANY LITTLE GIRLS, I grew up wanting to be a nurse and a teacher—yep, both at the same time. I was painfully shy. I was also empathic. I picked up easily on other people's "stuff." I would feel in my body any aches or pains that other people might be feeling in their bodies. Because of this, I was accused of being "too sensitive" by nearly everyone who crossed my path.

When I was fourteen years old, I laid my hands on my grandmother, who was very ill, and I prayed for help so that my hands might heal her. I had never even *heard* the word *Reiki*, yet somehow, I innately knew we had the power to channel energy to heal others.

Often, as a kid, I lived in my own little world, daydreaming about the life I would have someday. I knew there was more to life than the day-to-day mundane routine I saw everyone living; yet I had no idea how to get there—wherever *there* was.

And then I arrived. To the "there" so many speak of. I wasn't the nurse or the teacher I'd dreamed of as a child, but I had my university degree and a full-time job, which was a blessing considering I graduated in the thick of the recession. But most days, I would slink down into my chair at work, willing the time to pass by quickly. Going to work every day not only felt like a chore, it felt like it was sucking the life right out of me. I was breathing, but I wasn't living. What could I do?

On a whim, I signed up for a Reiki course.

I had only heard about Reiki once before. I knew that Reiki was a complementary therapy for healing both emotional and physical pain and it was about setting the intention to use the universal energy for someone's highest good.

I took the class, and after my attunement to Reiki Level I, my energy shifted and my world changed. It was kind of like an earthquake had rocked my world and everything in it shifted immensely. Only...no external shaking—but *inner* change.

With some Reiki education and practice under my belt, I was beginning to feel more alive. But I was still stuck in that pesky, soul-sucking day job. Again, what could I do?

On a whim, I decided to create my website, *The Daily Awe.* The intention was to post something daily that would put people in awe.

I began giving Reiki treatment sessions to clients. During the sessions, I began to see their aura colors and to receive intuitive messages for and about them. When I created *The*

Daily Awe, I had no idea I could do intuitive readings for other people and I hadn't the slightest clue what to do with being an empath, aside from trying to use it to win poker games. True story! Thanks to my blog, I met a couple of incredible teachers who taught me how to do intuitive readings and how to use my empathic abilities for the greater good.

If someone had told me even a year ago that I'd be doing intuitive readings for people, I would've looked at that person like he or she had two heads. Five years ago, I didn't even know what the word *Reiki* meant. Yet one baby step at a time, I arrived to where I am now, doing readings and healing others with Reiki. And I couldn't be happier.

I've found that inner guidance is a quiet thing. My discovery of Reiki and subsequently signing up for my Level I course was a calling.

Each of those "whims" of mine was the voice of my own divine inner guidance.

In a way, what I am doing now is no different than what I dreamed of as a kid. I am both a healer and a teacher rolled into one by providing Reiki and intuitive readings. I now share my knowledge of the world of Reiki with my students and those in my life. Being a Reiki Master/Teacher is far more than just a job—it is a way of life.

I now practice Reiki on clients several times a week. My most rewarding work is done with my local hospice chapter. Helping clients gracefully handle the side effects of chemotherapy with Reiki is one of the most profound blessings I've experienced in my life. Treating an ailing child with the Reiki energy opens my eyes and heart to what really matters most in life. I thank the universe every day for introducing me to the wonderful world of Reiki.

About the Contributor

Lindsay Curtis is a Reiki Master/Teacher and spiritual intuitive who blogs at *The Daily Awe*. She provides intuitive readings for those looking for insights on soul contracts, spirit guides, and their soul's purpose. Lindsay was born and raised in Central Pennsylvania and now lives in Toronto, Canada. She can be reached at lindsay@thedailyawe.com or at www.thedailyawe.com.

"As we were giving Reiki, I began to notice a tall mass of energy with swirling soft pink and green tendrils in the corner of the room to my right.... It felt loving."

—Yvonne P. Gleason

Embracing My Friend

BY YVONNE P. GLEASON

IT'S FUNNY HOW SOMETIMES, out of the blue, we suddenly remember a dear friend whom we haven't seen for years. This happened to me one day as I was teaching a small Reiki class. I had been talking about Reiki for pets and usually I talk about my cat and Reiki, but this time, I began to talk about my friend and his dogs. Actually, I ended up talking more about my friend, which was a bit unusual. My friend had a generous heart and though I hadn't seen him for years, I still remembered his hugs and special way of embracing all kinds of people. He had many who loved him.

It wasn't long after the Reiki class ended that I got a call that my friend was in the hospital in intensive care. It was an issue with his heart. My husband and I headed for the hospital. Once we arrived, our beloved friend greeted us with a broad smile, elated to see us. We hugged him and then began to give him Reiki with the hope that it would help him through the health crisis.

As we were giving Reiki, I began to notice a tall mass of energy with swirling soft pink and green tendrils in the corner of the room to my right. I didn't know exactly what it was and I asked my husband if he saw it. He said he didn't but that he felt something there. I'd thought perhaps it was an angelic energy or the energy of a Reiki guide. It felt loving.

We continued to give Reiki for a couple of days and our friend's condition improved. We left the hospital with high hopes. We were happy to have seen our friend and grateful that he was appreciative of the Reiki.

Only a few days later, we learned that he had passed away. We were very sad but I knew we had done our best to help him. Clearly, this was one of those times when Reiki hadn't helped the recipient improve physically.

Over the next week or so, I kept wondering about the energy mass I'd seen in the corner of the hospital room. Finally, I asked a mutual friend who is intuitive. He told me it was a portal that was lovingly being created for our friend to pass through upon his transition. Then he told me he had seen that same energy mass a week earlier, remotely, as a premonition, when he'd found out about our friend's hospital stay. He added that giving our friend the Reiki helped prepare him to go into the portal to the other side of the veil, when the time was right. I was surprised to learn that portals can sometimes be seen and that they are so beautiful.

Later, I shared this with my husband and we were grateful to have been able to give the Reiki as preparation for our friend's transition. I was also grateful for the experience of seeing a portal for the first time, and I believe it was the Reiki that helped me to do that.

Though I miss my dear friend, it helps to know that just as he had embraced so many others in his life, the Reiki we gave embraced him, preparing him for the portal, so that he could pass gently through its welcoming light.

"Though I didn't know a lot about Reiki, I decided to try a Reiki treatment session because I had a problem that would not go away..."

—RUTA SEVO

Spiritual Helping Hands

BY RUTA SEVO

T HOUGH I DIDN'T KNOW a lot about Reiki, I decided to try a Reiki treatment session because I had a problem that would not go away, and medical people had no clue as to its root cause nor considered it a health problem. There was fluid gathering in my abdomen that showed up on ultrasounds, and what felt like lumps inside the abdomen. Several doctors had inspected me and I had several ultrasounds. There was discreet muttering among the medical people but they did not tell me what they saw except for the interior reservoir of fluid. Serious diseases were ruled out.

Women in my family had a history of uterine fibroids, and long ago I had had an ectopic pregnancy with no known cause. However, it disturbed me because I could feel one of the lumps growing and even protruding on the side opposite to the appendix. It was nearly the size of a hard-boiled egg and I could feel it getting bigger.

Before I scheduled a Reiki treatment session, I had an intuitive reading done to see if there were any past life connections to my current physical symptoms. I learned that in my past lives, I was twice attacked in my abdomen. One incident involved a man who was furious at my pregnancy and he cut out my uterus. I survived but lived on in poor health. The second incident was during the Crusades, when a Christian soldier attacked me and my children and drove a sword through my belly, killing me.

I shared both of these stories with my Reiki practitioner when I arrived for my treatment session.

During my Reiki session, I experienced a light feeling like weightlessness and could feel my arms levitate. I pictured snow falling, with my body getting lighter and formless, dissipating upward to merge with the snow.

My deceased younger brother came into my consciousness. In his life, he had been a fisherman, who often cleaned the fish he had caught, on the shore of a lake or stream. Now, in the middle of my Reiki session, his hands, which had been so adept at cleaning fish, were now working deftly with my "entrails", rubbing them clean of debris, and taking things out that did not belong and discarding them. He was purifying my intestines and putting them back. I was grateful for the spiritual helping hands.

At one point during the session, I also saw my recently deceased mother. She looked upon me with love. Her presence was a nurturing experience.

In the course of the following week, something wonderful happened. The lump in my abdomen that had stuck out, reduced from the size of an egg to the size of an almond. Then it disappeared. I felt less bloated and may have lost some weight (which I was working on anyway). My libido gradually returned.

From my experience I perceive Reiki to be a two-person "trance" where the energy coming through the practitioner interacts with the energy of the subject and balances or improves the energy to create a healthy flow in the subject.

The Reiki treatment session was a significantly beneficial experience and I look forward to another session and the physical or spiritual benefits that it may bring.

About the Contributor

Ruta Sevo, PhD, is currently a writer of fiction and a consultant on the status of women in science and engineering. She retired from a position as Senior Program Director at the National Science Foundation in 2006. She also worked as an information technology analyst, planner, and manager, and as a systems librarian.

"I sensed that my friend was in trouble....I closed my eyes and simultaneously sent some of the Reiki to my friend while I continued to receive the Reiki for myself."

—Yvonne P. Gleason

A Gift from the Universe

BY YVONNE P. GLEASON

I HAD SCHEDULED A REIKI TREATMENT session for myself because I knew I needed to relax. I'd been struggling with an issue from my past, and I was searching for the lessons I felt I needed to learn from that issue. During the session, I received an "understanding" around the issue, but as it turned out, that wasn't the only thing that I received during my Reiki session.

As the Reiki session began, I settled into the safety and peace of the environment and nestled into a rainbow-colored blanket that was draped over my body. There was a small fountain nearby, and I began to be lulled by the sound of the stream of water gently splashing onto the pebbles below.

As the session progressed, an emanation of energy in the form of green discs began streaming from my brow chakra. As the discs grew larger and larger, I became very relaxed.

During the session, sometimes I felt heat from my practitioner's hands; sometimes I did not. Sometimes I felt "floaty," and then that sensation would ebb.

Then something unexpected happened. A picture of my friend's face suddenly zoomed in front of my face. It repeated twice. I sensed that my friend was in trouble. Not big trouble. Just something "not great" was happening to him. I checked the clock. It was 2:05. Then I closed my eyes and simultaneously sent some of the Reiki to my friend while I continued to receive the Reiki for myself.

After the session, I called my friend right away. I asked him if he was OK.

He said he'd been pulled over by the police because he'd forgotten to put the new registration sticker on his license plate. He was given a fine.

I asked him if he knew what time that had happened. He said it was about five minutes after two o'clock. He had been running late getting back to the office after being on lunch break.

I told him that while I was receiving Reiki, his face had zoomed in front of mine and I had known something was wrong. Then I told him that I had sent him some Reiki.

He said the Reiki must have helped because he had been much calmer than he normally would have been in a situation like that. He said, "It felt like a cloak of peace had come over me." Then he said, "Thank you for helping me to stay calm."

I felt so grateful for receiving the message so that I could send the Reiki to my friend.

I'm forever grateful for the connection to the universal energy of Reiki that is available to help us every day.

May you enjoy your unique journey into personal and spiritual growth.

Questions for Self-Reflection

Have I been gentle and loving with myself today?
With others?

Do I need to release worry so that I can be available
in the present moment?

Do I need to make more "me-time" or quiet time
with my Higher Power to just be in the stillness?

Are there things in my life that frustrate me
that I'd like to feel differently about?

Do I put my best effort into my work?
Is the quality of the work I do a reflection of my values?

*Before sleep, or during the day, are there things I do
that help me feel calm?*

What are some things I feel grateful for in my life?

*What are some ways I would like to continue to grow
or move forward in my life?*

More about Reiki

Qualities of Reiki

✦ Reiki is a form of complementary care, and it works well with other modalities or treatments.

✦ Reiki is noninvasive and gentle, and the benefits may be profound.

✦ Reiki helps to create a community of well-being for self and others through Reiki shares or Reiki meet-ups.

✦ Reiki works with the intention for "the very highest and best" for the Reiki recipient.

✦ Reiki has the ability to shift a recipient's energy to a more uplifted state, allowing for positive change in daily life.

✦ Reiki promotes deep relaxation. Having a period of deep relaxation can be beneficial to the body, mind, and spirit.

✦ Reiki allows one to have a quiet time with Source or Higher Power.

Places That Offer Reiki

- ✦ Hospitals
- ✦ Hospices
- ✦ AIDS Clinics
- ✦ Cancer Treatment Centers
- ✦ Physical Therapists' Offices
- ✦ Chiropractic Centers
- ✦ Veterinary Clinics
- ✦ Animal Shelters

Many nurses are taking Reiki training and then teaching other nurses and health-care professionals so that they can give Reiki as an additional modality to help patients.

Reiki and Intuition

WHEN GIVING REIKI, as practitioners, we may work intuitively. Over time, our intuition may increase and we may become more confident in intuitively knowing where to go, on or above the recipient's body, to give Reiki.

If desired, Reiki can be a modality that helps us to develop our intuitive skills for problem-solving or helping a friend. Reiki can be helpful in this way not only for practitioners but for recipients too.

What is intuition?

Intuition has been referred to as "a gut feeling." Most of us have heard of "Mother's intuition," which allows a mom to know when her child is in trouble even from afar. The good news is that we don't have to be a mom to be intuitive. We may naturally sense if a friend or loved one is in need of a helping hand. Then we can call and tell him or her, "I was thinking about you. Is everything

OK?" Or we can just ask for Source or Higher Power to send that person love and light for his or her well-being.

Listening to our intuition can help us make better decisions in our daily lives and help us to solve problems that come up at the workplace.

There are other modalities besides Reiki that have been helpful in increasing intuition, such as certain types of meditation and yoga.

If we become aware of the intuitive part of the mind, and use it along with the logical part of the mind, this gives us the ability to approach situations with a balanced viewpoint.

Reiki and Meditation

MANY HAVE FOUND that Reiki and meditation go well together. There is at least one particular Reiki training program that has meditations built into the curriculum.

There are various styles of meditation, and each of us may resonate with one style over another. Reiki meditations may involve movement, or meditations can be more static.

Many find that they enjoy incorporating self-Reiki into their meditation sessions by placing their hands on a chakra or a part of the body that needs some extra energy while meditating.

Both Reiki and meditation can be beneficial for creating greater clarity and focus in our daily lives.

Distance Reiki for People and Their Beloved Pets

WE CAN SEND REIKI to our loved ones even though they may be many states or countries apart from us.

Distance Reiki is universal energy that joins with our intention for the highest good of the recipient. Thoughts are energy. Our intention is energy. Energy is dynamic and it can travel to help our loved ones far away.

Distance Reiki works for our beloved pets too! Because animals are usually naturally intuitive, they may easily receive distance Reiki.

Distance Reiki can be sent to help create positive energy for an upcoming event or to help heal our feelings around a past event.

We can even help manifest our goals with distance Reiki.

Reiki for Personal and Spiritual Growth

REIKI CAN BE a wonderful modality to help recipients find the next step on their personal and spiritual paths.

Reiki brings deep relaxation which promotes focus and clarity in daily life. With clear thinking, we can more easily make daily decisions, as well as the longer-ranging decisions about our future.

During a Reiki session, recipients might have a realization about an issue they had been concerned about. They may begin to find solutions to a problem, or find an understanding about something they had been confused about.

In our daily lives, sometimes we have a lot of "mental chatter" and our minds are always going. Because Reiki allows recipients to deeply relax and energetically balance the body and the mind, answers to questions may easily rise to the surface.

Often, over a period of time, Reiki recipients begin to feel a deeper peace within, and it is from this balanced place that they begin to find more happiness and inner guidance for their well-being.

Frequently Asked Questions

Q: Can I ever get too much Reiki or not enough Reiki in a treatment session?

A: The good news is that the Reiki goes where it needs to go for each individual and in the right amount for each individual. The practitioner has an idea of where it needs to go, but the Reiki comes from an intelligent Source, so what each person needs is what each person will receive. So, you're getting the exact amount you need at any given time.

Q: Sometimes when I'm receiving Reiki, I fall asleep and I feel I'm learning something important in a dream. But at the end of the session, when I wake up, I forget what the lesson is. How can I remember the lesson the next time I experience this?

A: Before your Reiki treatment session, you could ask Source/ Higher Power to help you remember what you learn during your session. Sometimes, as a recipient, we may need to learn something at a subconscious level. Once we relax and trust the process, if there is something we're meant to know, it may be revealed when the time is right.

Q: **If I'm receiving Reiki for personal growth regarding a specific issue, how many sessions do I need before this growth will start happening?**

A: Each person is different when it comes to experiencing growth or change through Reiki. Sometimes a deep-seated, long-standing issue may call for more frequent treatments in the beginning. It is very specific to each individual and is something the practitioner and recipient can discuss.

Q: **When I'm giving Reiki, sometimes my mind wanders and I think of things like *I need to get some food for dinner tonight*. Is this bad?**

A: It's not "bad" if your mind wanders. As practitioners, sometimes thoughts may come and go, and we notice them, and gently bring the mind back to the flow of Reiki.

Q: **What should I be thinking when I send Reiki to someone?**

A: Ideally, once you've set your intention, when you actually give the Reiki, it's a matter of just being the vessel for the energy to come through. You may notice certain qualities about the energy at different chakras or energy fields of the recipient. If you're working intuitively, you may just know where to go next in the energy fields or chakras. It's beneficial to keep relaxed, alert, and open so the energy can flow. Some practitioners say this is similar to how they feel when they meditate.

Q: **Sometimes when I give Reiki, I see a shimmering light next to me and feel a loving presence; how do I know if it's an angelic energy, a spirit guide, or my animal guide?**

A: Over time, you may be able to discern this. You may ask Source and see if you receive an answer. It isn't necessary to know exactly which energy it might be; just be thankful that you feel a loving, supportive presence to assist you as you give Reiki for the highest good of the recipient.

Q: **Can I send Reiki to my Reiki guides, or do they not need Reiki?**

A: Many practitioners send Reiki to their Reiki guides. It may not be a matter of the guides "needing" it, but they may appreciate that a loving energetic connection to them is being deepened.

Q: **I've asked my friend in Maryland to give me distance Reiki anytime she wants. I'm in Virginia, and sometimes I feel her giving me Reiki like a warm blanket of unconditional love that comes over me. Whenever I call** her and ask if she just gave me Reiki, it turns out that indeed she had sent me some Reiki. How is it possible that I could feel the Reiki from so far away?

A: Reiki is universal energy that joins with intention and travels to where we want it to go. It's nice when the recipient can feel that loving, healing energy being sent.

Q: Sometimes when I receive Reiki, the hands of my practitioner aren't very warm. Does that mean the Reiki isn't working?

A: The Reiki still is working. Although a Reiki recipient sometimes notices warmth coming from the practitioner's hands, it isn't always that way. It's different for each person.

Q: Do I have to do all the steps to prepare to give a Reiki treatment session?

A: It is suggested that practitioners follow the steps they've learned in class because it creates an inviting sanctuary of energy in the room and it allows Reiki to begin flowing through the practitioner. Some practitioners enjoy the process of preparing because it is like a quiet meditation time for them.

Q: When I'm at a Reiki share, sometimes there are two practitioners simultaneously giving me Reiki. Does that mean the Reiki is stronger than when I receive Reiki from just one practitioner?

A: Some recipients feel that the energy comes through more effectively when there are two practitioners giving Reiki. Others say it feels the same for them, whether it's one or more practitioners giving the Reiki. No matter how many people are sending Reiki at the same time, the recipient receives the appropriate amount of energy for him or her.

When two or more practitioners join their intention for the highest good of a recipient, it allows for an unconditionally loving connection to be created between the practitioners and the recipient. During the Reiki shares, it can be nice to have more than one practitioner holding good intentions for your well-being.

Q: Whenever my practitioner sends distance Reiki to my cat, Sheba, she is calmer around my other cat, Dorsey. Also, for several weeks after Sheba receives a distance Reiki session, she jumps in my lap more often and wants to be petted. I'm still a little skeptical about how distance Reiki could actually work—but Sheba seems to feel better after each session, so I keep getting sessions for her.

A: Most animals tend to be receptive to the Reiki whether it's hands-on Reiki or distance Reiki. Most animals have keen intuition as they often need it for survival in the wild. Usually, domesticated cats and dogs have keen intuition as well. Distance Reiki is universal energy that works with the practitioner's intention and establishes a connection to the recipient wherever he or she is located. Energy is dynamic and it can travel. Cats and dogs (and people too!) are able to receive Reiki from across a room, or across many states or countries. It sounds like Sheba may be reaping some benefits from her distance Reiki sessions.

Q: **Do special distance Reiki guides help to get the energy to me when I receive a distance Reiki treatment session?**

A: Before a practitioner sends Reiki, he or she may call upon Reiki guides for assistance, and the guides help send the Reiki to the recipient whether it is for in-person Reiki or distance Reiki. So, you'll receive the help of appropriate Reiki guides for your session.

Q: **Earlier this year I sent Reiki to the earth, its tectonic plates, and the core for calmness and well-being of our planet. But two weeks later there was a series of tornados in the Midwest that destroyed houses and hurt people, some of whom were children who died. Why didn't the Reiki work to prevent that destruction?**

A: The Reiki helps in ways that are needed at the time—ways that we sometimes don't see. When you sent Reiki to the earth, an unconditionally loving energy was sent to the planet, and more than likely, that energy was joined with others who may have been sending Reiki at the very same time that you were sending it.

The Reiki is received, but we might not know the details of how it's being utilized. This is where Reiki and expectations come into play. As difficult as it might be, when sending Reiki, it's suggested that practitioners let go of expectations or outcomes and set their intentions for the highest good of the recipient, and trust the process. Sometimes all of us need a gentle reminder to let go and let it flow.

Q: **I usually book my Reiki treatment session weeks in advance, but once I arrive for my session, sometimes I feel too restless to calm down and be still on the table.**

A: As a Reiki recipient, you are free to change position on the table as much or as little as you want. A practitioner can give the Reiki even when the recipient moves around. Sometimes, when a recipient is restless, he or she might want to sit in a chair to receive the Reiki.

Q: **Sometimes I do self-Reiki during my regular meditation sessions. Is it more effective to combine Reiki with the meditation?**

A: It's fine to combine self-Reiki with meditation. Each person has his or her own experience as to whether it feels more effective to combine the two modalities. It usually changes the experience of the meditation in some way. Some people find the combination very beneficial.

Q: **I really like giving Reiki using breath, and my girlfriend says it's like a gentle wave that travels from head to toe. So, when I'm out of town, I send her distance Reiki and do some inhalations and exhalations during the session.**

Is it a good idea to use breath to help send the Reiki during a distance Reiki session?

A: One of the great things about distance Reiki is that all of the various methods of sending Reiki for in-person treatment sessions may also be utilized in distance Reiki sessions. Incorporating breath into a distance Reiki session also may help with focus during the session.

About the Editor

YVONNE P. GLEASON is a certified Reiki Master/Teacher of Usui Reiki and Karuna Reiki®. She practices in Northern Virginia, giving Reiki treatment sessions and offering Reiki training with a focus on Reiki for women. In addition, she offers distance Reiki sessions for pets.

Having come into Reiki as a child, she has worked with Reiki for many years with beneficial outcomes for herself and for others. Yvonne uses self-Reiki daily to revitalize her energy and help her discern more clearly the next step to take on her own path. Yvonne also teaches a Reiki meditation class which incorporates Reiki into meditations.

"Reiki is a journey that has helped me to grow and continues to help me grow in many ways. I believe that giving Reiki and teaching Reiki helps others to remember their innate connection to the supportive universal energy. I'm grateful to be able to share the amazing modality of Reiki with others so that they may have an opportunity to grow in their personal and spiritual lives."

Glossary

The following are definitions for terms mentioned in several of the *Reiki Journeys* stories.

attunement. A Reiki attunement is part of the Reiki training program. An attunement is a transfer of energy from Source, through the Reiki Master to the student. It allows for the appropriate quality of energy to be utilized by the Reiki student for a specific level or degree of Reiki.

aura. The aura is comprised of layers of energy fields around our physical body that depict the energy emanating from our physical body, emotions, thoughts, and spiritual connection (see "energy fields").

chakras. Chakras are energy centers or vortexes of energy that reside along the spine, at the top of the head, and at the base of the spine. These spirals of energy circulate the necessary life force needed for the corresponding areas of the body.

Each chakra is associated with a color. Each has a specific purpose and meaning.

energy fields. Fields of energy surround our physical body and make up the aura. The fields correspond to our physical body, emotions, thoughts, and movements to higher consciousness.

Reiki degrees or levels. Reiki is taught in different levels with the Master Level or Master Degree being the final level.

Reiki guides. Reiki guides may be called upon by the practitioner before giving Reiki, to assist in the Reiki treatment session. Examples of Reiki guides would be Dr. Usui, the founder of the Usui Reiki system; Mrs. Takata, who brought Reiki to the Western world; or Dr. Hayashi, who was a well-respected energy worker.

Reiki share. A Reiki share is a gathering or meet-up for the purpose of giving and receiving Reiki. Sometimes participants bring food to share at the beginning, and then everyone teams up to give and receive Reiki on the Reiki tables. Reiki shares can provide a time to practice Reiki skills and often healings or growth opportunities occur.

sensei. A general definition of sensei is "master" or "teacher." Sensei is a Japanese word which literally means "person born before another." The term is used to show respect to someone who has achieved a certain level of mastery in an art form or some other skill. For example, the founder of the Usui Reiki system is Dr. Usui or Usui-Sensei.

Usui Reiki Training

Level 1 through Master Level

Intensive courses offer a mix of academic and hands-on learning. Listed below are some of the topics covered.

Reiki 1:

- ✦ The history of Reiki
- ✦ Elements of the human energy system
- ✦ How Reiki works
- ✦ How to use Reiki for personal and spiritual growth, healing, clarity, and to assist others
- ✦ Scanning and beaming

Reiki 11:

- ✦ How to send distance Reiki
- ✦ The Reiki Second Degree symbols and their use
- ✦ Reiki using breath
- ✦ Techniques for cleansing your space, grounding, and focusing

Advanced Reiki:

✦ Two types of Reiki meditations to strengthen your ability to focus and expand consciousness
✦ How to create a crystal grid to send Reiki continuously
✦ Aura clearing technique using breath to remove blockages in the energy fields

Master Reiki:

✦ Ancient healing symbol and how it can be used with Reiki
✦ How to give attunements
✦ How to give a healing attunement, which assists in helping others
✦ The Reiki Master Meditation to harmonize your chakras
✦ The values and ethics of a Reiki Master

For more details, go to www.reikinova.com.

Karuna Reiki®
Training With a Focus
on Compassionate
Action

This class offers a mix of academic and hands-on learning.
Among the topics covered are:

✦ The definition and origin of Karuna Reiki®

✦ Karuna Reiki® symbols, purpose of each, and how to
activate them

✦ How to prepare for and give Karuna Reiki®
treatments

✦ A meditation technique to promote deep inner
healing

✦ Specific tones and chants to create a higher energy
frequency during treatments

For more details, go to www.reikinova.com.

Reiki Meditation and Mindfulness Meditation Classes

CERTIFIED MINDFULNESS MEDITATION instructor, Yvonne Gleason, offers Reiki meditation classes for relaxation and stress reduction, mental clarity to improve focus in daily life, and personal and spiritual growth. Mindfulness meditation is taught as an introduction to meditation and it provides a solid foundation for Reiki meditation.

Classes are a mix of academic and hands-on learning:

Mindfulness Meditation Class

Among the topics covered are:

+ History of meditation
+ Techniques to help with distractions during meditation sessions
+ Meditation and the mind-body relationship
+ Seated meditations versus active meditations

Reiki Meditation Class

Among the topics covered are:

✦ Incorporating Reiki into seated meditations
✦ Reiki and active meditations (walking meditations, movement meditations)
✦ Incorporating chanting or toning into Reiki meditations
✦ Creating your own Reiki meditation

For more details, go to www.reikinova.com.

Notes

Notes

Notes

Notes

Notes

Notes

Notes

Notes

Notes

Notes

CPSIA information can be obtained at www.ICGtesting.com
Printed in the USA
BVOW04s0350290115

385529BV00009B/97/P